CREATIVE EDUCATION

EARLY SPORTS BOOKS

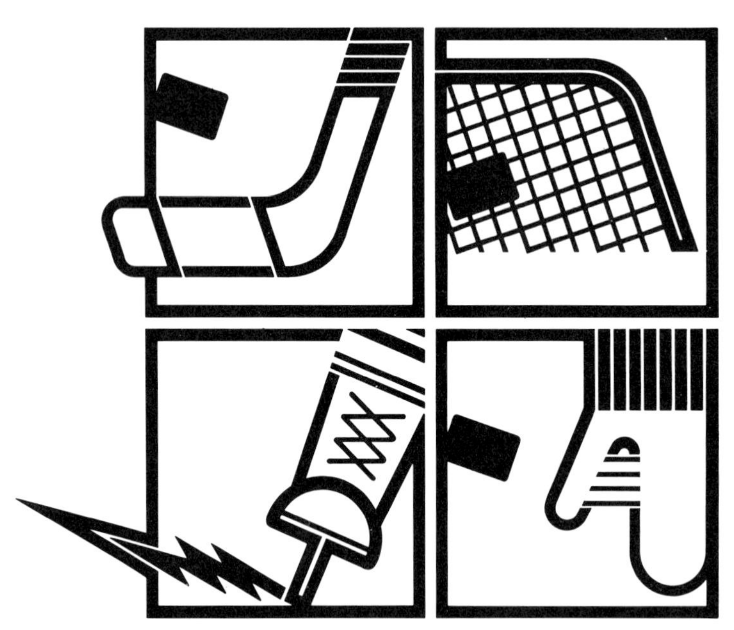

MEET THE GOALIES

by Linda Thomas

photographs from the National Hockey League

creative education

childrens press

Published by Creative Educational Society, Inc., 123 South Broad Street, Mankato, Minnesota 56001 Copyright © 1976 by Creative Educational Society, Inc. International copyrights reserved in all countries. No part of this book may be reproduced in any form without written permission from the publisher. Printed in the United States.

Library of Congress Cataloging in Publication Data
Thomas, Linda   Meet the goalies.
SUMMARY: Biographical sketches of four hockey goalies:
Ken Dryden, Tony Esposito, Bernie Parent, and Gilles Gilbert.
1. Hockey—Biography—Juvenile literature.
2. National Hockey League—Biography—Juvenile literature.
[1. Hockey—Biography]   I. Title.
GV848.5.A1M637   796.9'62'0922   [B]   [920]   76-21057
ISBN 0-87191-533-2

KEN DRYDEN

Ken Dryden started playing for the Montreal Canadiens during the last few weeks of the 1970-71 season. The Canadiens won the rest of their games that year.

Ken also played in the play-offs. The first play-off game was against the Boston Bruins. Ken was able to stop Bobby Orr and Phil Esposito as the Canadiens won in an amazing upset.

He also helped hold off the Minnesota North Stars in the semi-finals.

In the finals the Canadiens faced the Chicago Black Hawks. The series was tied at three games a piece. In the final game, Ken let Chicago have 2 goals but no more. He stopped everything they sent to him. Montreal won the Stanley Cup. Ken won the Conn Smythe Trophy as the Most Valuable Player of the Play-offs.

The next season he won the Calder Trophy as Rookie of the Year. He was able to qualify for this because he had not played in enough games during the previous season.

29

In the 1972-73 season Ken helped Montreal conquer first place and win the Stanley Cup. Ken won the Vezina Trophy as the leading goalie.

Ken did not play in the 1973-74 season due to a disagreement over his salary.

He returned in the 1974-75 season ready to play. Montreal finished in first place. They lost in the play-off semi-finals to the Buffalo Sabres. Ken was listed as the sixth leading goaltender in the NHL.

In the 1975-76 season Ken won the Vezina Trophy again with the best goals-against average in the NHL. With Ken Dryden goaltending, Montreal won the Stanley Cup for the 19th time.

TONY ESPOSITO

The Montreal Canadiens introduced Tony Esposito to the National Hockey League in the 1967-68 season. He started in ten games. Montreal lost only two of those games.

During the play-offs he sat on the sidelines as a reserve goalie. Shortly after the play-offs, Montreal traded Tony to the Chicago Black Hawks. They had finished in last place.

Tony helped the Black Hawks reach first place in the East Division during the 1969-70 season. He won the Calder Trophy as Rookie of the Year and the Vezina Trophy for goalie. The Black Hawks had allowed the fewest goals in the NHL that season. Tony set a new record for shut-outs with 15.

The Black Hawks kept the first place spot in the West Division for the next three seasons. Tony worked hard helping the Black Hawks keep this record.

He shared the Vezina Trophy with another Black Hawk goalie during the 1971-72 season. In the 1973-74 season he tied for it with the goalie of the Philadelphia Flyers, Bernie Parent.

During the last few seasons the Black Hawks have not made first place. But Tony Esposito is still listed as one of the leading goaltenders in the NHL.

Bernie Parent was drafted by the Boston Bruins. He played in 35 games during the 1965-66 season. The team finished in last place.

In the 1966-67 season he only played in 17 games. When the NHL added six new teams in 1967, the Philadelphia Flyers drafted Bernie Parent.

The Flyers did not give Bernie the top goalie
position during the 1967-68 season. This was given to
Doug Favell. The Flyers finished the year in first place
in the West Division.

Bernie did not play much until Favell was unable to
play during the play-offs. Even though he had a
record play-off average of 1.60, the Flyers were
defeated by St. Louis.

SHER-WooD

The Flyers traded Bernie during the 1970-71 season to the Toronto Maple Leafs. Bernie left the Maple Leafs to join the World Hockey Association. He only played in the WHA for one season.

Bernie returned to the Philadelphia Flyers in the 1973-74 season. Bernie and the Flyers defensemen were the toughest in the NHL. Bernie played in 73 games. He had a 1.89 average with 12 shutouts. Bernie and Tony Esposito of the Chicago Black Hawks tied for the Vezina Trophy for the leading goalkeeper.

The Flyers finished in first place in the West Division. They went on to win their first Stanley Cup. Bernie Parent received the Conn Smythe Trophy as the Most Valuable Player in the play-offs. He was also named to the All-Star team.

In the 1974-75 season the Flyers again finished in first place. Bernie won the Vezina Trophy that year with a goals-against average of 2.03.

The Flyers finished off the Buffalo Sabres to capture the Stanley Cup for the second year in a row. Bernie won the Conn Smythe Trophy for the second year in a row. He had four shutouts and had allowed only 29 goals in 15 games. He was again selected for the All-Star team.

Bernie started the 1975-76 season in traction. But when the season ended, it looked like another Stanley Cup for the Flyers. Then they played the Montreal Canadiens in the finals. Montreal beat the Flyers in four games. They won the first three games by only one goal. The last game ended with a score of 5-3. The Philadelphia Flyers and their goalie, Bernie Parent are not easy!

HOOD COUNTY PUBLIC LIBRARY

GILLES GILBERT

Gilles Gilbert is not the leading goalkeeper in the National Hockey League — yet.

Gilles started with the Minnesota North Stars during the 1969-70 season. He only played in one game. During that game he allowed 6 goals! For the next few seasons, Gilles did not play very much.

The North Stars traded Gilles in 1973 to the Boston Bruins. Gilles played in 54 games during the 1973-74 season. He had improved. In fact he finished the season with a 2.95 average. Boston ended the season by placing first in the East Division. The Bruins went on to defeat Toronto and Chicago in the play-offs. For the Stanley Cup finals the Bruins played the Philadelphia Flyers. The Flyers won the Stanley Cup.

THOMS
SHERWOOD

The Bruins did not stay on top in the 1974-75 season. Even though Bobby Orr and Phil Esposito of the Bruins were the leading scorers in the NHL, the Bruins were defeated in the first round of the play-offs by Chicago.

The most interesting team in the National Hockey League in the 1975-76 season was the Boston Bruins. The Bruins lost their top players. Phil Esposito was traded. Brad Park was injured. Bobby Orr was out for the season in November. Still, Boston made it all the way to the semi-finals in the play-offs. One of the main reasons for Boston's record was their goal-keeper, Gilles Gilbert.

MEET THE COACHES
MEET THE LINEBACKERS
MEET THE RECEIVERS
MEET THE QUARTERBACKS
MEET THE RUNNING BACKS
MEET THE DEFENSIVE LINEMEN

MEET THE WINGMEN
MEET THE CENTERS
MEET THE DEFENSEMEN
MEET THE GOALIES

MEET THE INFIELDERS
MEET THE CATCHERS
MEET THE MANAGERS
MEET THE HITTERS
MEET THE PITCHERS